Here are five boys and girls from Britain, France, Spain, Italy and Germany, ready to help you make new friends on the beach! It's easy to follow: just look at the flags, both on the beach clothes and in the flag circles. Around the pages, each word or phrase is shown in English first, and then in other languages. The speech bubbles show how the words and phrases might be used among friends.

Sharing a few words with each other can be great fun! Enjoy trying new languages – and enjoy your holiday.

With grateful thanks to:
Bruno and Remo Ciuffardi
Patricia Sofroniew
Brigitte Beresford Davies
Henar Herrero
Audrey Reeder

My holiday friends ● Meine Urlaubsfreunde ● Mes amis d

Name....................... Name....................... Nom........................

Address .... Adresse .... Adresse ....

Keep in touch! ● Schreib doch mal! ● Ecris

...vacances • Miei amici di vacanze • Mis amigos en vacaciones

'Bye!

Tschüs!

Nome...................... Nombre..................

A bientôt!

....
Indirizzo .... Dirección ....

Ciao!

....

....

¡Adiós!

....

...moi! • Fatti sentire! • ¡Escríbeme!

LAAKSONEN & PIRKKALA
PB 125 SF-20101 TURKU
FINLAND

Would you like to make more new friends from around the world?

It's exciting to find out about life in other countries by exchanging letters, ideas, drawings, photos and much more with someone of your own age and interests.

IYS, the International Youth Service, is the world's largest pen-friend organisation, founded in 1952. IYS arranges foreign pen-friends for young people of 10 years of age and upwards. For information on IYS and details of how their service works, you can write to them at the following address:

**International Youth Service
P B 125, SF-20101 Turku 10
Finland.**

First published in 1993 by
Bright Books

Concept, Design and Text:
©Bright Books Ltd, UK.
All rights reserved.

Illustrations:
© Natalie Bould

Typeset by Set Two, Ely, Cambs.
Printed in Hong Kong by Wing King Tong